# ELYSIAN MOON

## PEACEFUL AND PERFECT

# POOJAA

Copyright © Poojaa
All Rights Reserved.

ISBN 979-888591873-2

# Contents

# Contents

# Contents

# Acknowledgements

With the God grace I am compiling these anthologies.

I would like to give a heartily thank to all the dear co-authors who gave their best in the completion of this book. To be honest, without them it would not be possible to organize this anthology.

At Last I would like to thank my all well-wishers who supported me directly and indirectly through their suggestion.

Special Thanks to-

Kashish Publication for giving me this opportunity.

Poojaa

# Disclaimer

This anthology is a work of fiction. Names, character, places,events and incidents are either the products of the author's imagination or used in a fictitious manner. Any resemblance to actual persons, living or dead, or actual events is purely coincidental. All the content in this book is unique, and it belongs solely to co- authors.

The writers have tried their best to make the content of this book original and plagiarism free.

In case of any detection of Plagiarised content, neither the publishing house, nor the compiler is to be held responsible. The writer is to be held responsible for his/her own content.

# About Us

Kashish Publications is a growing platform for all the budding writers to fulfill their dream. It is founded by Kashish Soni,a budding writer who believe that writing is the magic to heal one's heart.

*"YOU DREAM,WE ACCOMPLISHED!"*

You can contact us for solo publishing or for compiling a one of our own.

Instagram id- @kashish_publications

Gmail- sonikashish004@gmail.com

# About The Project Head

He is Mr. Krishna Bagdi. He hails from Madhya Pradesh. He is an entrepreneur and a digital business consultant.

He is founder of Dream World Publication , Dwp Writing castle and Helping Hand Foundation.

Part of Cc Sports Academy and Team Grow more.

He has a keen interest in writing and photography.

"When you have fire of dreams in your eyes, I am serving you all here so that each writer would be appreciated when someone reads a book."

# About The Compiler

Poojaa ( WhiteAura) lives in Uttar Pradesh, India. She is a proud mother of two children. She has a zeal to do with her imagination.

She wants to give wings to her emotions and thoughts. For effectuate this she wield with words.

# Compiler's Desk

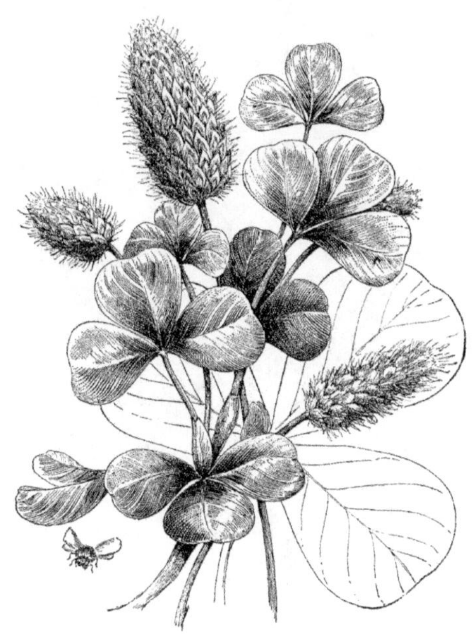

# 1. Poojaa

**Moon light**

When the days are tight
And in the darkest night,
I wish for the moon
With the full of light..

I looked at the sky
Where no stars at sight,
But the moon appears so bright
That illuminates the darkness of night...

# Co-author's Desk

# 2. Ankita Sarkar

Ankita Sarkar is a girl from Jamshedpur. She did her graduation on Hospitality Management and now majoring in Child Psychology. She has published her own book and has been a part of many anthology books. She express her feelings through words.

**Simplicity is complex**
It is very simple to be happy,
But it is very difficult to be selfless,
It is simple to show-off,
But it is very difficult to be natural,
It is simple to be kind,
But it is very difficult to be kind,
It is simple to be forgive,
But it is very difficult to forget,
It is simple to be love,
But it is difficult to maintain.

# 3. Ankita Nahar

#AKII#@@@ Ankita Nahar is originally from Ajmer, Rajasthan. She is always excited to write as well as always finds comfort in words. She writes her thoughts and whatever she has learned from her life, experiences she has taken in her compositions.This makes her compositions very emotional and influential. Which attracts a lot of readers. She wants to take this medium further. You can read her creations on Instagram @naharankita1.

It's a problem
or is it happy
does not matter
I often get lost
in that lonely corner of my mind
where there is no one except me
There are many such people in my mind
but someone in that corner
Can't find even after searching
And don't know yourself
how much do i talk
who doesn't tell anyone
they all go there
burden all my own
come down there
always going to that corner of the mind

pain is only
but always coming back
are only relaxed.

# 4. Athira. A

Co-author Athira. A is a young poetess from Ernakulam, Kerala State. She has completed her Bachelors in Science stream from St. Teresa's College, Ernakulam. She has been writing poems for 15 years as her passion.Athira is the compiler of poetry anthology 'Camaraderie' and 'Euphoria'. Book reading and reviewing is also her major hobby. Email :- athiraorminnu@gmail.com

**The Holy Christmas Eve**

Once again, winter has arrived;
And along with it has brought
Myriad memories of yester year,
Those this mind craves to replay.
A warm grin is born on my lips,
On reminiscing the fun and frolic,
You and me had made together
On holy Christmas eve of last year.
Singing 'Jingle Bells' and dancing,
We had made the whole day lively;
And the chilly night was spent
By tasting toothsome cake and wine.
Today, the holy eve has arrived again;
But Alas! I am spending it all alone,
While you are fighting to guard nation,
With gun in arms and life at stake

# 5. Nazia Tul Fatah

The name of our angel is Nazia Tul Fatah. She lives in Bangladesh with her parents. She is studying at botany Department in Rajbari govt College. She is a publisher of an English magazine. She is a YouTuber. She is a motivator. She is a writer of sixty plus books.

**Moonlit night**

I love to do maditation. I meditative myself by hearing 432 hz frequency music. I love to do telepathy. And im succefull telepath, connected with alien. When i meditated, i feel like moonshine, the light of star, coldness of clouds at night. I feel river sound, rain sound in my mind. I love piano. I cant play piano but i love it. A lot of stars on my sky are sparkling. Peace is islam. Allah gives me peace in my mind. I hear wave of seas. I hear chreeping of birds. I feel warm of smooth sun light. I feel cold wind of open sky. Its all about peace. Love is peaceful. Love is parents. Love is smile. Smile is precious than anything. A childs smile is valuable. A child is blessing of Allah. I love Allah. He created us. He has given everything we need. When i recited quran, i feel peace. If we do good work, we will get peace in afterlife and also in this life. So we should pray to Allah. We should pray salah, read Hadith and quran.

# 6. Sohini Ghosh

She's sohini Ghosh. She's from the city of joy Kolkata. She's 17 years old. She's a writer by passion. She is a motivator and dancer too. She's the founder of a writing community words of heart and Co founder of writers amulet.

***SCREAMS IN DREAMS***

Can't you listen to my silent screams?
They're louder than the voice they echo in my dreams.
Behind the mask of life that carries a smile,
Exists a darkest journey that goes on miles after miles.

I am screaming for hundreds of years,
Thinking of fears it gives me tears,
My voice always falls into deaf ears,
They know the amount of pain I bear.

How can they hear these silent screams in my life!?
They can't meet the truth if I say I'm fine,
Theres no words to speak,
As my soul always feels weak,
Because of the thinking skills of the society is so cheap.
But I have been staying in my grip.

How can I explain them how exactly I feel,

Every moment my heart silently screams,

It's just like suffocation in a mist,

It's the way I hold your hand,

Someday it disappears like a band,

Some moments of life that's dissolved in sand.

I can't explain how extreme I feel,

So I hold myself to shut the mouth and silently screams.

# 7. Harshita Verma

Co-author Harshita Verma is a writer from Lucknow. She has completed her graduation in commerce stream. She has been writing poetry for the last few years as her passion. She wants to be a novelist in future.

**Time**

Existing in the world but not enjoying
Xen feelings in the heart but not listening
Imbibing the changes of daily life
Surviving the struggles of daily basis
The life lived was a mess
Not realising the importance
The time flying swiftly
Wasting moments of precious life
Now it is all changes
Today living to the fullest that is life
Enter the zone of happiness
Near your heart and true self
Come closer to the God that created you
Enter into the sanctuary of love and live
Enjoying each moment of life
The time brings tremendous changes
Imbibe these changes in life
Live life freely with no worries.

# 8. Idhaya Bhardwaj

Hello folks! Thank you for sparing your time to read my work. I write because that's the only way I know how to explain the world what's in my mind without having to give reasons for it.
I hope you like what I've written.
Happy reading:)

On lazy afternoons I entertain myself,
I think about whatever comes to mind,
About petrichorial smell,
And pretty branches of adenium intertwined.
Today a peculiar mist has set on my heart,
Because today I thought,
Aren't houses tombs of the living?
Isn't closure just a myth?
Doesn't the lingering ghost,
Of the dead's touch haunt us?
Wouldn't people melt if only they could see,
Faces of others everytime they turn around?
Like a flowing river it comes to mind,
And it takes just a branch to turn it's direction,
To a place from where you can never comeback.
Because who has ever gone back from realisations and thoughts?
They say living is a tricky game,
Were we asked for approval of participation,

Or were we just thrown on the board to play?

I know you're wondering what is it that I've been saying, but come on,

don't you talk the same way to yourself? Like an inexplicable poetry?

# 9. Vinay Verma

He ia Vinay Verma

He is from Uttarakhand

He is 17 years old boy who loves to write.

**The biggest test of human life - :**

Who takes the most difficult test of a man? From my experience every person's toughest test is taken by time. If the person does not take decision at the right time then time never forgives that person. Because time is very cruel. It never shows pity on anyone. Time can spoil everything of the person but we cannot spoil anything of the time. A person who is unable to handle himself at the right time then time gives him very little chance to recover or we can say it does not give time at all. Time is hard. It doesn't look rich or poor. It only sees who can walk with it? Those who walk with time are supported by the time. This is a test of life that everyone knows or does not know. Time is very cruel. It breaks or joins a person. Sometimes it even takes away the life. A wrong decision of a person forces him to burn in the fire of repentance for the lifetime. When a person takes right and welfare decision and works hard to accomplish it then he lives only for achieving high position. That is why everyone should start to prepare for a better future from the first day of the year. Time will also support us in it. Whether they would be students in the field of or anyone else in the field of education or whoever they would be. Whatever the sources are in our hands at present we have to start from that. Utilizing time is a noble and welfare decision in this new year. We should not let it go by our hands. Only then we will be able to make our future on the right time.

# 10. Har Deepansh Bahadur Sinha

He is Har Deepansh Bahadur Sinha .

He belongs to Lucknow,UP.

He is a research scholar of Oceanography and has done masters in Geography from National Post Graduate College.

Completed his schooling from Study Hall.

His hobbies are art , listening to music , cooking & loads of driving.

His interest areas are Astronomy, Writing, Photography & Travelling a lot.

**Heyy , That's Me**

He is a confident and joyful personality

Also don't take his life casually,

Regularly practicing for the progress

Definitely one day he will attain success.

Extremely bold and vibrant by nature

Exclusively a very passionate creature,

Pouring and serving humanity selflessly

Aiming to spread love tremendously.

Never ever cheated in relations

Since he respects the connections,

Honestly he is sarcastic and hilarious

But towards knowledge he is curious.

Always ready to take challenges

He is well aware of Imbalances,
Also he is a brilliant poet
Don't dare to ask him for a duet.
Usually he doesn't gets exhausted
Reliable source and can be trusted,
Savior among his beloved friends
Independent and setting up trends.
Not afraid of moving in dark
He himself has got immense spark,
And the story goes on and on.

# 11. Arpita Saxena

Hi myself arpita I'm teacher by profession and loves to read novels and fond of content writing and planning to do PhD as well.

I see innumerable stories
Building up different facets of life .
I see different hues .Ever changing every second .
I see the mysterious ways of binding and letting go.
I see sky the infinite .Ever powerful. Ever generous .
I see life life unfold its untold stories .
I see the unseen .Enigmatic .
And therefore sky fascinates me

# 12. Afrin Ruksar

Afrin Ruksar is from Jharkhand and by Profession - Owner of a Book Company(Golden Letters Publication), CEO & Founder of Golden Letters, Project Head Compiler, College Student, Writer, Editor, Singer, Shayar, Poet, Tejaswini Project Member. Primary School - Saraswati Shishu Vidhya Mandir T.Tangar . High School - U.C.Girls' High School Jampani . +2 Inter College - St.Mary's Inter College Samtoli,Simdega. Subject - I.sc (Science) College - St. Xavier's College Simdega . Subject - B.A (English Literature) Hobby - Singing, reading, traveling, learning to new things, writing,drwaing etc. Ambition - I want to become a Popular writer, Professor and a Playback Singer also. Written Books - झारखण्ड की मिट्टी, साहित्यिक अरमान, उड़ारयिाँ, साहित्यिक राहें, साहित्यिक उत्कर्ष, कुटुंब, लफ़्ज़ तेरे मेरे, दहलीज़, अधूरी दास्ता, ये है चाहतें, सपनों की सीढ़ी, The Unfolded Words, Shadows of Life, The Modern Testament of Scrittura,Indian etc.

**Up in the Air : A Poem**
What people think about me,
I really don't care,
Good persons tell a true,
And bad persons are liar,
Fly on the sky at the night,
And look at the side of moon and star,
When my family tention,
I want to be all of happiness buyer,

When I wanna see to some child,
Who is a great player,
I don't find that child,
Now all child play pubg and free fire,
I wanna fulfill my dreams,
I move on by the small small stair,
I don't think negative,
Because I know wits is my power,
When anyone gain the knowledge,
Then they make wisdom tower at the atmosphere,
When someone hurt me a lot,
Then I keep silent and only prayer,
Whenever I win anything,
Then I listen the voice of clapping and cheer,
When I do good work,
Then I feel up in the air...

# 13. AVNISHA

A medical student and writer .

Best known for her Instagram page

" @my_diaryof_emotions "

She is a introvert in nature , assiduous and a beautiful soul without selfishness .

She is co-author of many books .

She likes dancing , playing badminton and chess.

**"MOON AND SUN "**

If I am moon then you are my sun!

Both are completely different ,

But can't stay away ,

Don't want to lose eachother ,

And Now they have come together such that like a beautiful evening .

If I am moon then you are my sun !

The sun light up moon's life ,

The moon glows brighten in the darkest hours of sun,

The moon only glows because it's reflecting of the sun.

If I am moon then you are my sun!

How beautifully the moon let's the sunshine throughout the day and the sun let's the moon glimmer at night!

If I am moon then you are my sun !

When the sun and the moon, both meet each other in the evening ,

There is a very pleasant atmosphere,

The both get together in such a way that it is very difficult to separate the two.

# 14. Priya Das

She is Priya Das belongs from a Bengali family of Northeast India (Assam), born on 30th September. She is passionate about writing and paintings. She is a trained artist, calligrapher and a published writer. She loves to play with beautiful words and fond of reading books.Her writings portray a contrast of nature and a glimpse of reality of life .At present she is pursuing Bsc, and coauthor of 200+ anthologies.

**Stolen Heart:**

Everytime I see you,

I get lost in the dense forest of your love.

The lush green fields soon turned into the fairy land of love.

Thousands of days I have waited for your love.

Your soft cold touch makes my clock to stop at every moment.

The charm of your beautiful smile makes the shining moon blush....

Your beauty embrace the glittering stars.

My heart ,beats with the rhythm of your kindness. ....

I want to walk thousands of miles in the shimmering night of bright moonlight.

Holding your hands in the cool breeze,and enjoying the view of the crimson sunset in the velvety sky.

I will not let anything to take you away...

I have loved you thousands of times in my dreams....

Maybe the shooting stars has granted my wish to be yours...

# 15. Deep

He is professionally Accountant, He resides in Sirsa Haryana, A Poet by Nature. he is interested writing a Poem to embrace his Love for Someone whom he loved. Apart from this. He love to Listen to Soft Sad Music. Watching cartoon....

**Promise of promises**
Promises ... which cannot be fulfilled,
If you did something, I did something.
Promises ... which cannot be fulfilled
Sometimes there was a shortage of time, sometimes he himself was very fast.
Promises ... which the Wafa could not,
Sometimes the relationship was advocated and sometimes they were beyond themselves.
Promises ... that cannot exist
Sometimes they got carried away in emotions and sometimes they forgot them.
Promises ... which can never be on their own,
Sometimes he was with the feelings, sometimes he was not with the feelings.
Promises… which cannot be steel,
Sometimes broken for myself,
sometimes for a relationship.
Promises ... which cannot live up to the point,

Sometimes the tears flowed and sometimes the ink was scattered on the pages.

# 16. Payal Kamdi

Payal Kamdi from Maharashtra.

A girl with passion in writing mess with her heart and mind. The picking of ink and fell down of paper which cames along shadow. She is penning her thoughts by penname Nityashree. She believes writing helps to concrete thoughts and manifest faster. Being a self lover she is binder of relationships too.

Love can loose you but gives you hope of finding stars she convinced.

A friend at a date
became a mate
He is little shy
quietly makes a fly
Stunning sound
everything around
a friend in a date
was my favourite date
during first meeting
I felt love at first sight
a simple thread
smile everyone's heart
make me fall in his art.

# 17. Soniya Varghese

Soniya Varghese is a writer filled with her own euphoria. She is a person who remains euphoric to see the kindred and emotions evoked around her. She is an author who handles mostly romantic themes and fun thrillers which is both for teens and adults. Especially anyone who have once fallen in love in their life. Whenever she writes she takes a part from her own life. Her writings reflects all that she had experienced in her life. Anyone who reads all her writings can connect it with her life. Instagram: soniya__ varghese, Facebook: Soniya Varghese, Twitter: @SoniyaVarghese8

**Those silent nights**

There were a lot of scary nights. Everytime I saw a bad dream I always thought of you and if it was then I'd call you. You were the one thing which made my mind calm. Even if night were filled with darkness you always filled it with light. Not only you've filled it with light but also you have created a whole new atmosphere. I love the way you smile at me when I share my scary dreams with you. I always sat alone lonely in the corner of my room waiting for you to shine through my window sills. I was always sitting there silently waiting for you to give me company so that you'd be able to make my mind calm. It's all because of that elysian moon that shone bright and made my mind calm in all my scary and silent nights.

# 18. Anushka Jain

My name is Anushka
I am leo and 14years old
My head is my favourite swimming poop
I love reading fiction novels and I hope u loved reading mine.

Some believe,
Money is the key,
Others in relief,
Say it's harmony.
Peace is security.
Freedom to be me.
I can't guarantee,
But it's my priority.
Chase happiness,
You won't go back fruitless.
I'll be honest,
And keep my promise.
Let me complete,
It is friendship and love.
I'll repeat,
Peace is all the above

# 19. M.Gopika

M.Gopika, a 20 year old girl hailing from Kadaladi, Ramanathapuram District. D/O: D.Muniyasamy-Mangaiyarkarasi. She was born on 23 September 2000. She is a crazy writer and a budding artist. She loves to paint and make craft work. She performs many online and offline performances in poetry. She started her journey as a tamil poetry writer a long time ago. But now she started her new journey as a English writer some months back. Most of her poem's will inspire you to bring your best in you. Her write ups are simple and small, but the meanings and the pain are deeper like the deep sea. She penned her thoughts directly from her heart. Insta id : crazy_gops

**Kargil War**

Pakistan started the war,
without no one not knowing!
India has seen a lot of war's,
but our Army's never seen to be tired,
To defend our country and
protect us from dangerous situations!
I want to salute from the
bottom of my heart!
I want to give my full respect
to those who leave their
families and kids,
for our families -to sleep

peacefully in their night's!

# 20. Deesha Soni

Deesha Soni..a Post Graduate and M.phil adorns the hat of a multitasker of an educationist,artist,poet,photographer,author , blogger,homemaker,wife and mother...

She has 10 years experience in the field of Education as a Professor and Coordinator.Deesha has various publications to her credit in national and international levels.

Deesha has various published works to her credit... she has two books published on Amazon... named 'Just thoughts' and 'Random thoughts on pandemic'..Kindle edition and more than 100 plus published works on various online platforms of .. Deesha has been twice nominated for Author of a week award by Storymirror and has also won various recognitions in penning stories and write-ups.. at National and International levels...

Deesha has various published works to her credit... she has two books published on Amazon... named 'Just thoughts' and 'Random thoughts on pandemic'..Kindle edition has also won many prizes in National and international levels in many write-ups...

Deesha has also published her works in 300 plus anthologies of multiple genres...

**Rule of the Britishers...**
The East India Company of Britishers sneaked into the port of India back in 1608...

A group of merchants...tried to seek monopoly in commerce and trade...

Thomas Row took permission from Emperor Jahangir to start a factory...

Gradually spread deep into Indian affairs.... adopted the policy of divide and rule...and destroying rulers and their royalty...

Warren Hastings ..the British governor took charge in Indian territories...

The British Government assumed full control on India... expanding their boundaries...

The Britishers destroyed the Indian industries to ruins...

And the Sone ki chidiya was killed in the Britishers evil doings...

They drained India and indians in their best possible attempt...

Towards India's world economic share .. and it's abundant resources..they had a tempt...

The Britishers squeezed every possible wealth from Indian nation...

To take back massive prosperity from our country was the Britishers sole notion...

Dogs and Indians not allowed....was labelled by them...

The Britishers ridiculed and exploited us Indians putting us to humiliation and shame...

Indians were slogged and made to work like labourers... servants and maids...

In famine... poverty and acute starvation. . none of the Britishers came to our aid...

Indian Economy was wiped out in terms of trade and politics...

The cruel and sly Britishers came reigned our ancestors... with British Government policies...

They ripped Indian territories into pieces...

The friction of India Pakistan still is the witness of scars and traces...

Had our ancestors not fought amongst themselves..in tiny groups...

The Britishers wouldn't have had dared to destroy our country with its control and troops....

We still fight in the name of caste creed and religion...

For we aren't aware that someone still may slyly want to control and rule on us as their secret mission....

# 21. Saqlain Saquib

Saqlain Saquib is Principal of Modern National Academy. He is a Bibliophilic person which brought him into the writing world. He writes confessional and dictional poetry and sometimes Writes on Love and Life Theme which is his best. He loves to learn new words and New Languages.

**"I was in and in the shore"**
I was in and in the shore
To revive my identity,
As a cherisher, as a praiser
Of my Almighty's Blessings.
A crab then bite me
On my left toe
As it finding its prey!
The prey was me but a large
I smiled but left the crab forwarded.
The thought my brain awakened
"Why we always cherish the joy not the sufferings?"
It's too blessing and life's delight!
As every 'day' comes after 'night',
As every 'darkness' fades away with 'light'
I, too smile and ready to play with kite!

# 22. Shuly Sabnam Hoque

I'm studying M.A. in English Literature.I am interested to write poems from my childhood.I like to read short stories,drama and the life stories of authors.My earnest desire is to be a writer in future.My hobbies are painting,reading books specially the life story of the authors,planting,composing poems,frame making etc.

**WINGS OF PROSPERITY**
Clouds fly, Birds fly but I can not...
You can view the world but I can not...
Wings have you But I haven't...
I have Desire to fly, to show you the world
And will take Time to make my own wings,
The Wings of Prosperity!
So, You are Shouting and Shouting
And Feeling I worry
But Remain I silent!
Lemme Take my own Time!
And One day you'll be chirping for me
One day you'll be showering on me.

# 23. Riya Richard R. L

Riya Richard R. L is a young, burgeoning writer in English. She has adored writing since her girlhood. She has a unique style and distinct modus operandi in her writings- poems, quotes, short stories, novels, etc... She has worked as a Co-author in 200+ anthologies. She is from Kanyakumari district, Tamil Nadu. She is now an undergraduate in Chemistry.

**SHATTERED PIECES**
Now, the world is full
Of violence and battles,
The land is filled with
Corpses of People,
The waters have become
Red due to Bloodshed,
Air is filled with noises of
The Firing of Guns,
The Blasting of Bombs,
The boom of Dynamites,
Ears become deaf on
Hearing the Cries,
Peace is nowhere to be seen
Peace has now been
Shattered into Pieces!

# 24. Bhavika Mehra

Bhavika Mehra is a 15 years old Delhi student in 11th grade. She is a calm and relaxed-minded being who brings happiness to others around her. She loves to jot down everything that comes to her mind. She is a writer as well as a dancer. She is much into Bollywood and watches everything from anime to movies and kdramas to web series.

**POEM - MOM**

She is the beauty and she is the queen,
Her shoulder is on which I can lean.
She is there for me anytime,
She is the sun who shines every time.
Lying to her goes in vain,
She is there with me when I am in pain.
The one who wakes up at midnight if I am ill,
And thereby, becomes my pill.
I love her with all my heart,
And I know that we can't be fallen apart.
Can't thank her enough for everything she does for me,
She has a million ways to make me glee.

# 25. Bhumika Mehra

Bhumika Mehra, a 15 years old student, is from Delhi. Alongside being a diligent and calm-minded individual, she additionally attempts to maintain a positive atmosphere around herself and her loved ones. Dancing and painting are her pastimes. She always thinks analytically and rationally while solving textual and real-life problems. If you want to contact her, here is her Instagram ID- @bhumika_mehra13.

And on her birthday, after waiting all day, she received a text at 11:52 p.m.
"Happy birthday, my sweetheart. I hope everything went great. I love you ", It said.
She burst into sobs the following minute.


** The ones who want to be your lasts matter more than anybody else since they know that your firsts will be many, but sometimes all you need is someone in the end. They are the ones who remind you that you are not alone; they are there for you. **

# 26. hindi

# 27. Urvashi Gupta

Urvashi (Phoenixxx) grew up in New Delhi, India turned M.T. Initially focusing on performing arts, and life. From her childhood she shows interest in writing and began writing short stories, poems and motivational quotes and many other writings. She is a explorer who love to explore the world in her style. Worked in many companies with different field backgrounds and become the Phoenixxx in today's writers world.

"Go on your path, even if you live for a day." "Never give up on a dream that you've been chasing almost your whole life…" "Even if I'm a little hurt it's okay." "If you can't fly, then run. Today we will survive. If you can't run, then walk.

U is for Uplifting, so inspiring

R is for Ravishing, an entrancing beauty

V is for Virtuous, living in righteousness

A is for Alluring, so attractive

S is for Spectacular, truly remarkable

H is for Humorous, sparkling wit

I is for Important, an asset to society

G is for Genteel, elegantly mannered

U is for Ultimate, just the best

P is for Picturesque, strikingly beautiful

T is for Tantalizing, thrilling the senses

A is for Alluring, so attractive

*** Moonlight fame and glories***

Fame And Glories By Moonlight

Is to find where you lie

And it seems, you're where that I'm

Somewhere in the distance you hear the snow crunching

You know it's great fun

Somewhere in the distance you see

The sound of a heartbreaker

You can hear the screams

All the corners in the road

You know you're right there

The way those winter days can lead to one of

Fame and glories by moonlight

You can hear the wind across the mesa

The look in your yellow eyes

A look of pride tying

All those moments of true devotion

To your front door

And you know you're right there

The way those winter days can lead to one of

Fame and glories by moonlight

You can hear the wind.

# 28. Sahil Hindustani

His name is Sahil Bhatnagar and writes under pen name Sahil Hindustani. Inspired by Dr Vishnu Saxena and Mirza Galib he started writing in 2004. He is co-author of over 100 anthologies author of one anthology and also his ten write-ups are published in newspapers and magazines.

**Dear**

I will always love you oh my dear
Don't hesitate, trust, please come near
I know you're scientist and I am writer
But your inner beauty made me lover
I don't care 'bout our age, creed or cast
I just know I love you & will never last
Forever and ever please stay with me
I'll be loyal to you and won't take fee
Just once say you too wanna marry me
I'll fulfill demands you'll order me

# 29. Anwesha Rath

Anwesha Rath,

A girl from small town used to see huge dreams now is working in anthologies is just 19 years old doing graduation her aim is just to take care of her parents as they cared for her till her dream is not writing poems but to share heartfelt message..

**Teary eyes..**
The tears which flows continuously
The pain feel randomly
The heart which feel the care
The red color of eyes
The fake blush and fake smile
The happiness
That changes into sadness
The sadness washed by the tears
The tears change feelings into madness
These can never be exchanged
These can never be expressed
These can only be known
These can only be understand
By the one
Who is suffering or who already suffered
They know
They know the purity and clarity

Of their tears
They know the reality of those teary eyes
Which whole night cries

# 30. Noor Tabassum

The name of the author is Noor Tabassum. Writing is her passion. She has participated in more than 200 anthologies as co author and has also written solo books called Sensibles and Twisted Firsts. She is a nature lover and loves to lead a simple life. She expresses all her feelings in her writings as she thinks it is the most powerful medium to communicate. She has won many writing competitions, and her articles have been published in many magazines too. She enjoys writing poems and short stories. Her stories have been published in the Times of India newspaper too. Her Instagram id is @noortabassumali123.

**TEASING MOON**

Slept in the dark, cold magical moonlit night,
On the red sand staring at the full-wide moon in my sight,
Unbelievable happiness had surrounded me left and right,
And my heart flew like an aimless kite.
Moon smiled at me and asked where was my knight?
Why was I sleeping alone on a romantic night?
Why was I not in his arms, hugging tight?
Did not my love have that magical might?
I stared at it and smilingly replied,
My darling had gone to pluck few stars in the night,
To decorate a necklace around my slender neck with pride,
He had gone to bring few exotic flowers, white,

To spread on my sleekly hair straight,
He had gone to get the brightness from the moon at height,
As he wants none to be more glowing with light.
Other than his darling cuddling by his side.

# 31. Pallavi Deepchand

A girl named Pallavi is from Mauritius. Writing is her passion and it helps her to express her feelings on paper and gives her inspiration for her daily life activities. She writes poems, articles and short-stories amongst others.

**Music**

heart filled with the emotion that cnt hide by eyes..

sparks my heart catching from the think of desiring of you..

could not match my intense behaviour while thinking of you..

way of making thoughts of you not come to my mind but it comes and surround my mind with your thoughts when the silent night hits the window besides the curtains I catch you in my dreams to feel you once and twice and again..

dreamy of the nights will sparking the heart beats the music with it flows...

my soul dances in the sounds of musical tones..

# 32. Priyadharshini Singaravel

Priyadharshini Singaravel is an upright person. She has passion of her life and thoughts. She loves music and she always embraces by BTS (Bulletproof scout boy band) and she always be passionate to all. She is not talented person but she is the fullest and aiming to break her records by herself.

**NEW MOON OF THE THIRD DAY**

do you know new moon? that never shines but as the third day of new moon is quite special. because, it will show up in the sky for three hours. after three hours it will get fade. even though the people will say its a aspicious star and if see on the time it will give us blessings....

why i am saying this?....any guess!

we will say that we are unlucky can't do anything properly and so on...just think after thinking give a try, you can make it. Only thinking of what you wanna do next won't help, make sure to give it a shot whatever it is. Giving a shot won't make you tipsy nor drunk, instead it will make you steady and more stable than who you are before. Moon never embarassed for being New Moon for a day. because it knows that it's going to shine more than it being used in a days.

If you got some time try to watch New moon not cause you can gain luck or such things ..just wath it ..you will get you understand what you wanna do next.

it's okay to be dark but it's not okay to be in dark.

No matter what how the life it is, it will definetly get better. it may take some time........but it will definetly last forever.

DO YOU KNOW?

Moon never fails to make up....a best thing to success is doing everything on time.

# 33. MURALIDHAR BANSAL

HE IS MURALIDHAR BANSAL FROM NEPAL. HE IS A BUSINESSMAN AT PRESENT. HE WAS INSPIRED TO WRITE AS A STUDENT SEEING THE ENVIRONMENT AROUND HIM. HE LOVES WRITING AS A HOBBY AND HE WANTS TO BE A GOOD AND RATIONAL BUSINSSSMAN.

A TEACHER IS THE ONE WHO TEACHES US. S/HE TEACHES WELL BUT IT IS IN OUR HAND HOW WE TAKE THE KNOWLEDGE. ITS ALWAYS A BLESSING TO HAVE A TEACHER IN LIFE.

A TEACHER IS NOT ONLY FOUND IN TEACHING INSTITUTIONS. PARENTS ARE THE FIRST TEACHERS WHO GIVE THE BASICS TO ENHANCE FUTURE.

YOU YOURSELF ARE A TEACHER BECAUSE WHATEVER YOU DO OR PERFORM, IS THE ACTION TAKEN BY THE MIND AND HEART. THE MIND AND HEART ARE THE BETTER TEACHERS IN LIFE.

A TEACHER IS JUST A WORD IN DICTIONARY RATHER S/HE IS THE MENTOR, DEVELOPER AND FUTURE MAKER OF HIS/HER STUDENTS.

# 34. Mrunmayi Dhage

I'm mrunmayi dhage Im from Mumbai
As I'm graphologist
Vedic maths teacher numerologist
Handwriting Teacher poet writer
Author pschyantrist handwriting specialist signature specialist social worker.

**Peace of mind??**
The strength of the mind brings aspect of life.
Joy is the essence of the completeness of happiness.
The confident is inside, it is within.
Action proven, when we achieve what we deserve.
A peaceful mind and a peaceful heart generate power.
To be peace with God and to our self is a great achievement.
To link in the world materially is only temporary
The world is full of lies and full of disturbance.
Always remind ourselves that all thing in the rolling universe
Is temporal. To live in peace is more enjoyable,
We views thoughts in mindwith the peaceful feeling in
The heart. Love the life in a simple way.
"Peace I leave to you, my peace I gave unto you", Says the Lord.

# 35. Jhilam Adhikary

Jhilam Adhikary is a student of English honors in Amity University, Kolkata. She wants to be a poet, writer, professor and activist in future. She is a poet and artist who loves anime. Her poems have been published several times in e-magazines like TechTouchTalk and in books like Kopfkino, Twinkling Verses, Shouganai, Stars of Scars, Eternal Love, Personified Thoughts, Seraphic Habromania and Journey: It never ends. You can follow her on her Instagram: @d_orange_pirates

**JEALOUSY**

I blamed beauty
For all that's wrong in me,
And the universe
For splitting me in two
Mercilessly.
The other universes won't let me
Be me and grieve in peace;
And to swallow my anger,
I'm not ready.
I'm the most beautiful
For no one else
Can dare be a part of my world,
It's a declaration.
Beauty forgot to speak

When time was right
And universe was cold and sober;
The raging warmth stabbed the sky
And I knew at once,
I wasn't beautiful enough yet.
Tore opened my flesh
And emerged from my chest
This other entity
Called inner beauty,
Red with my blood;
And was accepted immediately
Singing,
Boasting the cruelty of my heart.
I cannot exist for myself ever
Just the universe though
Not beauty
Rest is the façade that we all see.
I'm the universe, all over again
Unrecognizable,
Overshadowed,
My own beauty, the other soul
Who can't be kept in a cage
The claustrophobia, the bitter rage
For I'm alone.
The other's universes are angry
While my universe is here,
Waiting for me.
Beauty looking around
Beauty looking down

And I'm left
My jealousy has thus awakened,
To calm my universe down
Again.

# 36. Shubhanjali Nishad

Im shubhanjali nishad from kanpur up writing is my passion which is god gifted

With a calm nature, what do I want to say when I wake up every day in the morning, I want to thank God first, yes, believe that there is a flaw, not everyone is the same perfect.

How can I deny this leela of God, make thousand faces with thousand hands, make some beautiful and some less beautiful, but I am very lucky, I have made my parts complete, my heart is calm, we keep saying thank you to my God because He has made everyone visible with his own eyes, change the view, look at every person not by appearance, but by appearance.

If the eyes do not seem laughable, then go to God's and do some complaint chatter and see

# 37. Fahad Ashaie

Fahad Ashaie, a growing poet and writer from beautiful Kashmir valley . He has recently completed his M.A literature from University of Kashmir . He is the modern writer, having skills of writing with essence of postmodernism, classical, and metaphysical art.

Fahad Ashaie, is having hobbies of travelling , writing and gardening since childhood

His writing take us to the taste of modern Shakespeare , Eliot and John Donne. He has ability to write fiction , reality and consciousness.

He is presently Co Author in many national and international anthologies under the banner of Savan publication , Anshay Publication , The Opus coliseum. He is also the compiler of many anthologies.

**Thank Goodness**

Like branches of the trees

absorb water provenance their roots, Feeling afresh, you see how they retort stow from their shoots.

Like the oceans,dispersed at length adorn the clouds,

back to water drops eventually they fall.

Like the deeds of runs are commanded in the oceans,

ALL hearts get filled with gratitude for each of nature's counsellations.

# 38. Rachana Saha

Rachana Saha, a budding writer. She has a great interest and love in writing. She bleeds her feelings in her diary. She is in class 8 reading in St. Xavier's Institution. She is born and brought up in Kolkata. She is co-author of many anthologies and wants to write more. She is compiler of two books THE BLANK PAGE and BLEEDING METAPHOR. Other than writings, she has a great interest in drawing.

**《《The melodious soul》》** •
I will search for you
In the cloudless night
In the crowed place
And in the silent sky.
In the night light
And the lampshade
On the shore
And the hills of peace.
I wonder where
You could be now
For years my heart
Hasn't seeked out loud.
Longer since
We met each other,
Time has passed,

For you and me.
But I have learnt
To live without
The heavenize tune,
Still I love you infinite.

# 39. Javeria Saghir

"No doubt, passion comes before talent."
Javeria Saghir - from Lahore, Pakistan - is pursuing graduation in the field of chemistry from GCUF. Apart from study, she has a keen interest in creative writing, poetry, singing, and artwork. She began writing in 2020 and achieved several certificates and positions in online writing competitions. She is adaptive and a passionate dreamer who has a firm belief that consistency and hard work will enable her to attain the impossible and make her strong enough to sparkle the lives of others.

**"Love"**
Love is an emotion,
Makes not oblivious though having different places.
Love is loyalty,
Keeps you sitting in an open cage.
Love is a connection,
Unintentionally, etches into one's body to spark his soul.
Love is a trophy,
To get after submitting to its demand.
Love is an affiliation,
Enchants one achingly and piercingly.
Love is a demand,
Forces one to give up a part of own self.
Love is immortal,

With no fear of death in mind.

# 40. Aanushnaa Bandyopadhyay

Aanushnaa Bandyopadhyay is a girl from Kolkata, studying in St. Xavier's Institution, class 8. She loves showing her creativity through arts and wants to be a professional violinist and a great writer. She's currently the ambassador of Imprint Publication and the Founder of Inking Hearts Writing Community. She has worked as the compiler of three books, namely, "The Independent Pen", "The Saga of Love" and "Women, not Weak", among which two came in the top 100 bestselling books on Amazon. She had also been a co-author of 80+ anthologies and won many writing challenges held by various writing communities. @bandyopadhyay.aanushnaa_2020

**The Masked Visitor**

It was striking 1 at night. I was quite awake, studying for my annuals, that were starting from the next day. I was in so much pressure that I couldn't think anything other than books.

I was concentrated on my notes, when suddenly I heard a sound from the balcony. Thinking it must the street cat, I ignored it.

It was hardly five minutes, when my mother entered with my dinner. After having it, I thought it better to rest for a while, and then start again.

I was preparing to sleep, when suddenly I heard a light footstep from the balcony. Now, I knew it wasn't a cat! I turned off the lights in my room to see who was that in the balcony.

Luckily, my windows were covered with curtains, so even if then I peep out from a corner, the person won't be able to understand.

Turning on my table lamp, which was literally too dim when compared to the LED lights, I look out from the window, through a small side of a curtain.

Peeping outside, I saw a mysterious black masked man, dressed all in black suit as if black was his favourite colour...

Keeping aside my humour, he was searching for something in the balcony, I don't know what?

Like seriously, what would one search in my balcony, that only consists of some flower pots, a resting chair and a tea table?!

My eyes stuck to his actions, what he was doing, what he was looking for? After a while, he tried looking inside the window, I guess he wanted to check if anyone's observing him!

Seeing him looking attentively to every nook of the window, I just went to bed, covered myself with the blanket, and closed my eyes out of anxiety!

After staying like that for few minutes, I came out. But, he wasn't there! Though I was scared, I went to the balcony, and checked for him down in the streets, but he wasn't there...

# 41. Vinita Rajaram

Vinita Rajaram was born on 20 February, 1999. She is the omg books of record holder for copyrighting her solo book - Karma : A Boomerang. She is the co author in 12 anthologies.

**Gender indiscrimination**

It is 21<sup>st</sup> century, but then also there is discrimination between girls and boys. In every field men is dominating. Girls are not given equal rights as boys are given. Most of the girls are not allowed to choose the career of their choice. As soon as when they complete graduation, their parents get their daughters married. It is also seen that after marriage , most of the girls are allowed to do job which is totally injustice . Girls are blamed for their dressing sense. Instead why don't they teach their son how to behave with girls. There are very less rules for boys but in case of girls there are infinite number of rules. Girls are told to behave like this or behave like that why don't they tell the same thing to boys or men. It is sickening to think that the people still differentiate between girls and boys. Some girls or women can really achieve heights of success but they are pulled down by the society or by their own parents or friends. If they can't support their daughter then they also should not talk negative about their career choice. It's her choice. Nobody should interfere or they don't the rights to say what she should do in the terms of their career choice. It is high time right now and instead of always taunting girls what to wear and how to behave. The society should teach their son how to behave with a girl or a women.

# 42. Saniya Varghese

Saniya Varghese is a 13 year old girl who loves to overthink.
She loves superstitional characters.Most
of the works of hers are full of her imagination which
leads the reader to an amazing imaginary world and she's a published
co -author of more than 20 book and compiler of 3 . She prefer's to be
alone, in an imaginary world.
Instagram Id : _saniya_varghese_

**THE UNNOTICED WORLD**
The glistering stars, the glowing moon
The dark which could devour me
The chirping birds & the strong wind
Laying on the turf and staring blankly
While the whole world is busy
How perfect & peaceful night it is
Which goes unnoticed by us
Alone in this night, I don't feel
The need of anyone near me
Maybe I never tried to understand,
I wasn't alone all this time

# 43. Aiwa Antony

Aiwa antony
A simple teenager
Who's lost in a world of arts
A silent writer
She loves to sing as well.
No matter where ever she is.. There will be always a diary and a pen
with her

**When the sea of stars shine**
When I talk to the moon, my heart feels light
Even I look at the stars, I know I'm not alone anymore
There is so much about this darkness in this sky when the stars align
and make a constellation
There is a peace and there is silence, a comforting silence that pulls me
to a soft lullaby
The night is like a sea to go on a voyage for and never return
The winds and the clouds, the moon and the stars
Just me and my thoughts,
My words and the only listener
Noting all in my diary..
Maybe they are the only once who knows the things which i can't say
Just my dairy and the moon being my loyal companion feeling the
cold yet soft breeze touching my wet cheeks as if it's the only thing that
can stop me from draining more, as if out of all this is what you call

comfort.

# 44. Jennifer Okoro Chioma

Jennifer okoro chioma is a Nigeria writer and blogger. She is passionate about music and she loves catering. She is talented, creative and resourceful. She is filled with dreams and plans. She aspire to be a medical doctor.

**Peaceful and perfect**
A mid night hush
Without flaws
And silence that heals
Where broke pieces
Glue together
To a perfect structure
The waves of ocean
Perfect and peaceful
The sounds of calmness

# 45. Khyati Sahrawat

Khyati Sahrawat is a 15 year old girl who was born in Uttar Pradesh and has been brought up in the valley of Dehradun which is widely known for its picturesque landscapes. She has always been intrigued by the idea of finding oneself in the midst of all the chaos and confusion that inevitably surface our thoughts. She says that her heart beats for experiencing new things that require her to step out of her comfort zone. In her own words, she loves doing things to feed her soul even if she's not perfect at it ,be it writing a writer bio or the main content itself.

**Bleak Emptiness**
Scared of the human void that surrounds you,
Bawling your eyes out,
All that's there is a broken person in a forlorn crowd.
Tired of the aching nothingness that surrounds you,
You plunge deeper into an inner abyss to search for someone inside,
Bitterness and pain grips you tighter when you realise,
It's empty inside.
Superficially there's so much around
But under the surface there's nowhere you feel safe and sound.
A horrible ,crippling feeling of despair grips you tight,
You sense a hole gaping from the inside.
Your insides hurt under the gnawing pressure from this profound vacuum,

It's all so full yet so empty, all so hollow yet so heavy.
Helplessly running away from the loneliness that chases you,
You're faced with the bleak emptiness and cold walls that surrounds
you,
It's you and loneliness in the same sphere on edges quite far,
Together yet so far apart.
Your lungs are deflated of air everytime you face this ostensibly eternal
hollowness that hurls you into the dark,
But it's temporary and its a part of a vacant charcoal hour.

# 46. Kakutsthy

Kakutsthya is a 14 year old Indian writer who started writing when she was 7 only. She is a flight cadet so love and determination for the country is obvious to be in her. She writes novels, poems, articles and much more. She also owns a blogging website and is currently working on a novel. She is most active on her youtube channel where she publishes videos of poetry, read a book or write a novel with me, precisely anything related to literature every week and she also shares tips and tricks for young writers like her. Till now she has won best speaker award in numerous events and has published a lot of books, she also owns a writing community.

Our love is like bleeding hearts, I wish it could be roses though they too have thorns.

This adoration is toxic but indeed is bewitchingly magnificent.

I'm aware this devotion can't be compared to roses as thorns give ultimate and instant pain but this lethal desire is divine and gradual.

Am i actually a lowly creature that even you treat me as a stranger or maybe this fatal affection is deceiving me.

Your words mislead

and your actions cheat.

This alluring intimacy is prepotent, even reincarnations can't dominate these sentiments.

And in sooth, this adoration caused my heart to bleed.